DEDICATION

I dedicate this book to each person that has experienced hurt, trauma, rejection, disappointment, injustice, bankruptcy, foreclosure, dispossessory eviction, repossession, divorce, failure, defeat, anxiety, depression, suicidal thoughts, homelessness and loneliness.

If God did this book for me, my prayer for you is that he will do <u>even more</u> for you.
Ephesians 3:20

Index

THE COST OF BEING
CHOSEN

Chapter 1

"The Cost of being Chosen."

Chosen transforms and does not conform. Chosen believes, according to Philippians 1:6 (NKJV) that he who has begun a good work in me shall complete it until the day of Jesus Christ. Chosen operates, according to Ephesians 6:10 (NKJV), not in its might but in God's might. Chosen overcomes, according to Romans 12:21 (NKJV) is not overcome by evil but overcomes evil with good. Chosen overcomes evil with God.

Chosen Believes, Operates, and Overcomes.

The word of the Lord came to Jeremiah in the Book of Jeremiah Chapter 1 verse 5 (NKJV). God tells Jeremiah, before I formed you in your mother's womb I knew you.. Before you were born, I sanctified you and ordained you to be a prophet to the nations. Like Jeremiah God chose us before we were pushed out of eternity into time and space through a time capsule called our mother's womb... God chose us.

Not only did God choose us but he took the extra step of consecrating and appointing us to be his prophet to the nations, before we arrived here on earth. A prophet to the nations, yes a transformer to the nations. How are we going to transform nations? We are going to transform the nations as chosen people according to Philippians 2:1 (NKJV) with the mind of Christ.

"It is no longer going to be WWJD, What would Jesus do but it now becomes WDJD, What did Jesus do? For the chosen there is no such thing as random. Your very presence and ear to hear this word from God is not random. Even your situation, your circumstances, and the problems you are facing right now are not random.

The death, the divorce, the abuse, the job layoff and termination, the threats, the trauma, the kiss of betrayal, the embarrassment, the health scare, the character assassinations, the emptiness, and the attacks are not random but

"The Cost of being Chosen."

Could it be possible that God has brought you into this situation, into this circumstance, and right up to this red sea experience for such a time as this? My question to you is this, "What is it that God knows about you that you have yet to know about yourself, that he is allowing the enemy to engage you? Let me answer that for you, **"You are Chosen!"**

In the Book of Acts, Chapter 9 (NKJV) of our text we see Saul continuing to persecute and prosecute God's children, the men, and women of God.

We see Saul's boldness, arrogance, intent, and foresight in obtaining arrest warrants before he journeyed to Damascus. These arrest warrants gave him jurisdictional authority to arrest and bind God's children, the men, and women of God. Suddenly God changes Saul's plans, and Saul falls into the hands of an angry God. It is still a dangerous and terrible thing to fall into the hands of an angry God by messing with his chosen.

Blinded Saul, fallen Saul, by the hand of almighty God is now trembling, and bewildered. Saul says to the Lord, "What do you want me to do?" The Lord instructs Saul to arise and go to Judas's house. Notably, there is nothing we can do for the Lord sitting down. We must arise and follow God's instructions. While Saul was at Judas's house something happened. Saul begins to pray. While Saul was praying, the Lord appeared to Ananias. The Psalmist said in Psalms 56:9, the moment we pray the tide of the battle turns.

In the seen and unseen realm, God begins to turn things in our favor the moment we pray. The Lord instructs Ananias to go and pray for Saul with the laying on of hands, a prayer of recovery, sight to Saul's blinded eyes. In verses 13-14 Ananias responds to the Lord, with what he thinks about Saul's reputation and what he thinks about Saul.

In verse 15 the Lord tells Ananias, what you think and what anyone else thinks about Saul and his reputation does not matter to me because Saul is chosen. What matters to man does not matter to God. Like Saul, you have been chosen, to bear the name of Jesus in the hedges, highways, byways, the palaces, the kingdoms and to the nations.

In verse 16 the Lord says there is a cost to being chosen. Jesus knew "The Cost of being Chosen."   3

Jesus knew Saul would have to endure not only the natural seasons of fall, winter, spring and summer but Jesus also knew that he would have to endure the four (4) spiritual seasons of crucifixion, death, burial and resurrection.

The First Spiritual Season is Crucifixion.
- Crucified is to be put to death by nailing or binding the hands and feet to a cross and left for dead. *(Merriam-Webster)*

Many of you reading have been betrayed, shamed, humiliated, embarrassed, taken for granted, looked over, look down upon, scorned, misused and abused, bound by the low expectations of others, bound by the miss-takes of your past and nailed to the cross of heart break after heart break, many of you have even been stabbed in the heart and left for dead. This is:

"The Cost of being Chosen"

The Second Spiritual Season is Death.
- Death is the irreversible cessation of life functions. *(Merriam-Webster)*

Many of us have experienced or is experiencing the irreversible separation and permanent dissolution from folks that we thought we could not function without. We must learn in this spiritual season to walk with Jesus there are some people, places, and things that must die from our lives.

There are some relationships, mindsets, decisions, life choices that shouldn't be revived. If resuscitated, they will dilute and pollute the plan, purpose, and power of God for our lives. Some folks can be more harmful to you than cigarettes, crack, cocaine, hereon, meth and liquor.

In 1 Samuel 16:1, God told Samuel, stop lamenting over Saul who I have rejected. Fill your horn with oil (with gladness) and be on your way I have chosen another.

God's message to you is to stop lamenting over who he has rejected out of your life, fill your horn with gladness and be on your way. God has chosen another for you. When death of relationship, people, places or things has occurred there is no getting back to normal, it is now a new normal. This is:

"The Cost of being Chosen."

The Third Spiritual Season of Burial.
- The act of being buried.. interment. *(Merriam-Webster)*

Many of you have been eulogized and buried alive. Many of you have had final rites spoken over your life and then dirt thrown on your hopes, dirt thrown on your dreams, dirt thrown on your name, dirt thrown on your address, dirt thrown on your progress, dirt thrown on your ministry, dirt thrown on your marriage, dirt thrown on your spouse, dirt thrown on your children, dirt thrown on your divorce, dirt thrown decision, and dirt thrown on you in the middle of a crisis. This is:

"The Cost of being Chosen."

The Final Spiritual Season is Resurrection.
- The state of one risen from the dead. *(Merriam-Webster)*

This is the spiritual season where God giving us double for all our trouble, all our shame, all of our difficulty, all of our hardship, all of our separation, and all of our loses in the previous spiritual seasons of crucifixion, death and burial.

God restoring everything and every year that the cankerworm, palmerworm, and the locust had eaten and stolen, according to Joel 2:25.

Like Jesus and Paul, we must understand "The Cost of being Chosen."

Apostle Paul, in Hebrews Chapter 12 verses 1-2 (NKJV), wrote, let us run with endurance the race set out for us. verse 2. Let us fix our eyes on Jesus, the author and perfecter of our faith, who for the joy set before him endured the cross, ignoring its shame and is seated at the right hand of the throne of God.

No Cross, No Crown...

LET US PRAY

What is it, that God knows about you that you have yet
to know about yourself?

_____

_____

_____

_____

Ask God, What do you want me to do?
What are you willing to do for God?

_____

_____

_____

_____

What are the Four Spiritual Seasons that was discussed?
Which season are you presently in? Why do you feel that way?

CHOSEN

THE CALL OF BEING

Chapter 2

"The Call of Being Chosen!"

We are entering into the final stages of Christ's imminent return. There is chaos in the schools, in the streets, in the church, chaos in the community, at the bank, in our homes, in our government, in the nations and chaos even in our lives.

Our conduct displeases God so much so, that God is asking an Old Testament question to the New Testament church, found in Isaiah 59:16

Where are the Intercessors?

Where are those charged with crying aloud in prayer and sparing not in ministering to the lost, and the unsaved generations? Where are those charged with the equipping of new disciples as soldiers to be placed immediately onto the battlefield, fighting for the souls of future generations?

When God was asking where are my intercessors, he was asking, "Where are my chosen?"
Where are my chosen that when the enemy comes in like a flood? Where are my chosen to pray and intercede for the spirit of the Lord to intervene and raise a defense against the enemy?

Intercessory prayer gives God permission to act on our behalf. God is not a burglar, thief, or robber. God is not going to break in on us, steal our supplications and apprehend our problems.

God requires our permission to act on our behalf, to deal with our difficulties and defeat the challenges and the chaos. God's plan is to foil the diabolical plan, plot, scheme, tricks, strategies, and maneuvers of our enemy. God's chosen are his intercessors, his instruments and necessary tools dedicated by him to release the power, the authority, the spirit of God to intervene and dispossess our enemy through prayer.

I believe Jesus was saying to his chosen esoterically in the book of Matthew, 28th Chapter: Verse 18. All authority has been awarded to you, through me in heaven and on earth. Verse 19. "Go therefore" chosen and make disciples of all the nations, baptizing them in the name of the Father and of the Son and of the Holy Spirit. Verse 20. "Teaching" them to become chosen vessels and to observe all things that I have commanded you and lo, I am with you always chosen, even to the end of the age, "Amen."

Also, I believe God's eagle eye Prophet Isaiah was saying, esoterically to the Lord's chosen, in the book of Isaiah, 61st Chapter, the Spirit of the Lord God, is upon the chosen because the Lord has anointed his chosen to preach good tidings to the poor; he has sent his chosen to heal the brokenhearted, to proclaim liberty to the captives and the opening of the prison to those who are bound; to proclaim the acceptable year of the Lord, and the day of vengeance of our God; to comfort and console those who mourn in Zion to give them beauty for ashes, the oil of joy for mourning, the garment of praise for the spirit of heaviness, that they may be called chosen, the planting of the Lord, that he may be glorified. We are talking about...

"The Call of Being Chosen"

Matthew said in the book of Matthew, 22nd Chapter Verse 14. Many are called but few are chosen. What God is saying this day, is that many have been called but you have been chosen. Being chosen means that God has placed his distinction upon you.

- When you are called, the odds are against you but when you are chosen the odds are for you.
- When you are called, life is happening to you but when you are chosen life is happening for you.
- When you are called you are sick but when you are chosen you are healed fighting off sickness.
- When you are called you are depressed but when you are chosen you are unbothered fighting off depression.
- When you are called you are poor but when you are chosen you are rich, prosperous and successful fighting off poverty.
- When you are called, you are a good example not to follow but when you are chosen you are God's example to follow.
- When you are called, many things shall entangle your feet but when you are chosen none shall hold you fast.
- When you are called, you fall down but when you are chosen you get back up again.
- When you are called, you learn from your own miss-takes but when you are chosen you learn from the miss-takes of others.

In the First Book of Samuel 3rd Chapter, we see Samuel a young MIT (minister in training) being called into active duty by the Lord. Samuel was being called to be a faithful priest and prophet, a chosen vessel to do according to what was in God's heart and in God's mind.

You may ask for what purpose? We are called to be God's faithful representative and chosen vessel to do according to what is in God's heart and God's mind. Our scripture text said that God knew Samuel but Samuel did not know the Lord or the word of the Lord.

You may ask, "How could Samuel be a minister in training and not know the Lord or the revealed word of God?" Samuel did not know that before he was formed in his mother's womb, that he was consecrated, appointed, and ordained, to be God's prophet to the nations.

Samuel had been chosen and there was a promise to God that was hanging over his life that had not been revealed to Samuel. The promise was the spoken word of God out of his mother's mouth through prayer dedicating him back to God, found in the First Book of Samuel 1st Chapter verse 11.

Pastor Eli, perceived that the Lord was calling Samuel. A Pastor's call is to develop a spiritual ear to hear, "the call of being chosen," upon your life. Romans 10:14 says, "How can they hear without a preacher?"

Pastor Eli, was charged with developing Samuel's spiritual ear to hear the call of God on his life. Pastor Eli, tells Samuel when the Lord calls again, say speak Lord, your servant hears. Samuel does exactly what his Pastor tells him, and God begins to share with Samuel that he is about to do a new thing in the nation of Israel.

God says to Samuel, this new thing is going to be so big, so great, so unexpected and major that is going to shock and appall the people. You see, practicing sinners never expect God to judge or execute his judgment on them for their willful disobedience. We have grace and mercy mistaken. God is not extending grace and mercy for us to continue willfully sinning. I believe they call those, the sins of commission. God extends grace and mercy for us to and come out of the willful practice of sin, against God and against our bodies.

The people thought that Eli and Eli's sons had gotten away with their blatant wickedness. Unbeknownst to the people, God was simply being merciful. God was allowing them time to voluntarily turn themselves in, under the full custody of the holy spirit.

Like Eli and Eli's sons, we have not gotten by or away from the balanced scales of God's justice. The consequence of obedience is still blessings, and the consequence of disobedience is still curses. This is why God was calling Samuel. He was God's chosen vessel, and God's chosen representative. He was to usher in God's new thing and God's new day in Israel.

God wasn't going to continue to allow Eli and his son to make a mockery of the priesthood.

In the same manner God is calling us and America to be his chosen vessels. God is not going to continue to allow wickedness to make a mockery of his priesthood. God is not going to continue to allow wickedness to make a mockery of his grace and mercy. God said in Galatians 6th Chapter verse 7 (NLT) don't be misled-you cannot mock the justice of God. You will always harvest what you plant.

<u>What is the Justice of God?</u>

God said in Psalms 75:10, he is going to cut off the horn (which means strength) of the wicked and he is going increase the strength of the righteous. This is exactly what God did to Eli and his sons he cut off their strength. God exchanged his grace and mercy over their life for judgment against their lives.

When we respond to God he cuts off the strength of the wicked and does a new thing in our family, in our marriage, a new thing in our community, in our church, in our home, in our government, in our finances, a new thing in our nation, and a new thing even in our lives. This new thing is going to capture the ears and eyes (the attention) of the unsaved, the lost and the saved.

This new thing is going to be lifting, refreshing and at the same time mind blowing. The spectators and the speculators are going to be shocked and appalled. Some will even fall backward in their seat in disbelief that God has chosen you like Samuel, to usher in his "new" move from heaven to earth.

God said in First Corinthians 2nd Chapter verse 9. Eyes have not seen, nor ear heard, neither has it entered in the heart of man, the things which God has prepared for those who love him.

My question to you is this, what is it that the enemy knows about you, that you haven't figured out about yourself? Let me answer that for you, you have been chosen. Much of what you are going through right now has nothing to do with the enemy but everything to do with "the call of being chosen," upon your life.

The things that are happening in your life are not demonic but prophetic. In the movie the Matrix, Trinity tells Neo, "if you are the one, you can't die now." Trinity tells him, "Now get up!" This book has been sent this day by The Trinity, (The Father, The Son and the Holy Spirit) to tell you, you are chosen, and you can't die now. Get up!

Get up out of adultery, fornication, homosexuality, transsexuality, lust, depression, anxiety, fear, low self-esteem, suicidial thoughts, anguish, grief and answer God's call of being chosen. Stop sending God to voicemail. Stop worrying about what you don't have and trust God with what you do have. This journey doesn't require experience it requires God.This is:
<u>The Call of Being Chosen,"</u>

LET US PRAY

What is it that the enemy knows about you, that you haven't figured out about yourself?

_____

_____

_____

_____

"Ears to Hear"
How have you found ways to draw closer to God and learn His voice for yourself?

_____

_____

_____

_____

www.ingramcontent.com/pod-product-compliance
Lightning Source LLC
Chambersburg PA
CBHW041613120626
46551CB00002B/432